# Contents

## The Healing Process


1.) Spirit of Rejection Pg. 2

2.) People Pleasing Pg. 9

3.) Seeking Validation Pg. 13

4.) Depression & Anxiety Pg. 18

5.) What is Love? Teach Me Pg. 23

6.) Discover Your Wounds Pg. 29


## The Glow Up


7.) Overcome Fear of Rejection Pg.37

8.) Build Self Esteem Pg.41

9.) Take Care of Yourself Pg.47

10.) Create Healthy Relationships Pg.52

11.) What is Your Life Plan? Pg.63

12.) Glow Victoriously Pg. 66

# Spirit of Rejection

Rejection has a way of making us feel less than worthy more often than we would like to admit, and that's only if we're aware that it's part of our baggage. Often, we are rejected by the people around us and most are not sure how to process those feelings, so we hold on to the hurt not realizing that the pain forms into many different behavioral habits that results in a hardening of the heart. A lot of one's rejection issues comes from childhood, which would explain why we fail to manage our emotions on the maturity level we would need to understand what is happening to us mentally and emotionally.

How you were accepted and treated as a child conditioned you, sometimes negatively, especially if you did not feel or simply weren't accepted as a child. Rejection from parents, whether it's the mother or father both have their own outcome of mental neglect. It's the most common root of rejection and both are traumatizing. For example, I felt rejected and abandoned by my mother and was physically abused and molested by my father, so mentally you could imagine I was not as stable as I should have been growing up. Although we're going to get into how God saved me from the way rejection shaped me, we're not at the part yet. First let's break rejection down bit by bit, so that no one misses the deliverance they are about to receive because they're thinking "This isn't my story". Welp! Everyone has dealt with rejection and in some way shape or form it planted a seed somewhere in you. So, let's keep going.

Now, being rejected by your parents is not the best feeling in the world and no one deserves to feel that way. However, if we're going to be honest there's a very high percentage of people that suffer from rejection trauma and it started right at home. It's sad that, that's where it's starts, but it gets even sadder when you know that's not where it ends. Once the seed of rejection is planted it follows you everywhere, school, workplace, social groups and relationships. The reason why is because you begin to look for things in people you lacked growing up. You begin to shape yourself into whoever you believe they will accept just so you can feel accepted by that person and or group. It's a spiral effect that will result in you losing yourself in the process.

Fear of rejection and its partner fear of abandonment are the creators of a lot of hurt, bad decisions, people pleasers, validation seekers and even personality disorders in some cases.

Making bad decisions whether it's in life, our relationships or daily lives are sometimes the result of abandonment and rejection issues. Decisions in your life are shaped from things that either has happened, you don't want to happen or would like to happen. Rejection can cause you to have fear based thoughts that will have you creating false narratives in your mind. If I don't do this, then this person will do this and if I don't do that then they will leave me. Romantic relationship where one feels fear of abandonment will do things that are out of their character to keep a person even if it means losing themselves in the process. It can also cause a lot of unhealed wounds to surface, and you begin to show up in that relationship as a person you don't even recognize.

Rejection and abandonment issues in a relationship is not to be underestimated. Some look at it as something people should just get over, but it's not always that easy for everybody. It can be potentially dangerous and it also the reason behind a lot of abuse and worse cases. There have been many homicides committed because they found out or felt as though their person was going to leave them or betrayed them in some way. I know that may seem extreme, but I'm giving an example on how deep this can go.

These types of cases are from uncontrolled emotions, actually all abuse and murder cases are from uncontrolled emotions. The legal term is "heat of passion", it's a mental state provoked by rage or fear. It's so common that it is recognized as a defense in the court of law. Rage becomes leading emotion, revenge becomes the action, abandonment or some form of rejection was the motive, and death was the outcome. People have different triggers, and some people are far more scarred than others. Though all abandonment and rejection issues do not result into this, we can at least understand its importance to heal from it.

Romantic relationships are another trigger for some people, and they don't know it until they get in them. A person will drag a relationship simply because they fear being abandoned or rejected. They also don't want to feel like a failure, so they try to trick themselves into thinking everything is alright. There are people fighting to stay in a relationship they don't want to be in all because they don't want the person to leave them. You don't even care for the person or the relationship, you just see another person leaving your life, so, you go into panic mode based on trauma. It's not always the fear of losing the person, it's the fear of being left alone as well.

Some people truly have anxiety attacks after a breakup but because they aren't aware of their emotions and traumas, they confuse the anxiety attack with heartbreak. Most of the time your heart is not broken you're triggered. If they break up with you, you feel abandoned and if you want to break up with them you prolong it because it means you'll be alone again.

A breakup can bring up emotions from years ago as a child when you felt left behind. Maybe the seed was planted when possibly a parent left, and now you're triggered because you felt abandoned back then and now in your adult breakup you feel that you failed. A breakup of any kind is a trigger for a victim of rejection. You have programmed yourself to focus on the negative part of the departure because as a child that's all you knew was the person is gone. You were left with your thoughts and most of those thoughts were that the departure was somehow your fault. So, anytime a person leaves you, you feel as though it's your fault. You begin to think you could have done something better. If you are the one wanting to go, you'll make yourself believe you are giving up too soon and that maybe it's not so bad. Understanding the reason behind this form of thinking will help you pull the plug when you need to.

# People Pleasing

People pleasing is a trauma response from things that has negatively affected you in your past. Some people will go to unhealthy lengths to please those around them and that includes losing themselves and who they truly are in the process. People give up their dreams and their goals to do things that will make other people happy because that's what other people believe that's what they should be doing. Even doing things you just simply don't want to do or feel uncomfortable doing becomes second nature. You would rather be uncomfortable in what you do just to have this person around than to be temporarily uncomfortable in losing them. Not knowing when to say no is a great example, you would pretty much say yes to everything. You went from loving to help people to hating it all because you don't have boundaries. You must have respect for yourself, and you must know your limits.

We are so eager to make others happy that we don't see we are making ourselves miserable by spreading ourselves thin day after day. Before you know it, you have all these tasks, and favors you must do because you wanted to please everybody and just didn't know how to say "no". Then you get an attitude and frustrated and if you don't know how to control your emotions you get angry. Problem with you being angry is you feel guilty about it. You'll self-blame and make yourself feel bad for having feelings.

People pleasing will drain you, shape you into someone you're not and change your outlook on life. Think about it like this, whether it's you or someone you know, there's someone right now taking on a career to please their parents. Someone wakes up every morning doing something they don't want to do because it makes someone else proud. That is a miserable life to live, there will be nothing but depression and sadness in that person's life because they are not being fulfilled by living out someone else dream. There's a teenager right now applying to a college they don't want to attend because their parents want them close to home. Sure, as a parent I understand that, but as someone who understands development and personal growth, I know we must let go and let God.

There's someone tonight hosting an event at their home knowing they'd rather be alone watching tv on the couch eating snacks. Oh! Let's not get on the Aunty that wants you to forgive your toxic cousin, or whoever, because they family and you do it sacrificing your peace because it'll, please the elders at the next reunion.

"If me doing something for you makes me unhappy then I can't do it" and that's exactly what a lot of you reading this need to start saying. You were not put on this earth to please everybody, sweetheart you going learn that everybody is not going to like you or like what you're doing. The moment you begin to set some boundaries and start saying no you will see who's around you for you.

Learn to know your limits of what you can and can not handle. Saying no for your own mental health is self-care for you. You don't have to explain yourself either. Your grown self do not need to explain why you choose not to do what you are not up to doing. It's none of their business what you have going on and it's none of your business what they think about it. Unless, of course, you asked them, which will lead us right into our next topic.

## Seeking Validation

Yep, we went from coffee to tea because I need to fill you in on a little something. The validation you are seeking from whomever you're seeking it from nine times out of ten you don't need it. Being validated makes a person feel like they are doing good, especially a person that has felt rejected or as if they aren't good enough. Now, asking for advice when you need it is one thing, but seeking to be validated is seeking approval of you being you.

Seeking validation has ruined so many dreams, visions, altered some personalities and even canceled some prayers. Yes, I did say prayers. Why? How many times have you prayed to God for something, and He gave you the answer or the thing and because you don't know how to hush you told somebody and they talked you out of it. Whether it was an idea or even telling you your purpose, you ran off to ask somebody "could this really, be it?" as if God needed their stamp of approval on his word. God told you who you are, and you went to someone else to basically ask them if they agree and because they can't see in you what God sees in you, they convinced you otherwise.

You came up on a business idea, made all your plans, thought it all through, went to somebody to ask them what they think, and they tore it all down. You can't seek validation from a person that doesn't see your vision, you're asking for confirmation from a person that don't have the qualifications to confirm it. You don't trust yourself enough to believe that what you have will prosper into something beautiful because the unhealed trauma wounds you carry has molded you into thinking you aren't worthy of such greatness. Any decision you make you need someone to tell you, you've made the right one because without that you run scared in your mind.

I know it may seem as though that doesn't steam from a place of rejection, but the definition of rejection is the dismissing of a proposal, idea, etc. and rejection can be given by anyone to anyone. So, if growing up none of your ideas or suggestions was taken into consideration, if you didn't feel heard or seen, you will grow into an adult that will seek out the attention and approval they've always desired. Of course, when you stumble upon or do something great you want people to hear about it, everybody loves a congratulations, a high five, and the thrill of it all. See, the seek has become so natural that you have conditioned yourself to think you are simply asking for advice when really you are disguising the inner child within you screaming "hey, look at me mommy, look what I did", or "Dad, I found something I can do that'll make you proud." "What do you think" is really "Do you approve?" Your seeking in validation is really a seek for a pat on the back, but as adults it's not cute to be needy so we call it a second opinion.

You really telling your business because you need someone to tell you if you right or wrong, and if you're right you need the "good job" that'll come along with it. Every time you seek you taint, because you run the risk of not hearing what you want to hear. The bigger problem is the people you're looking to be validated by need to be validated themselves. A circle of people looking to the next person for clarity and willing to change their whole point of view because someone else disapprove of it.

Seeking approval in everything you do in life will have you stuck looking right at the same people who disapproved of your idea because they too sought out for approval and didn't get theirs either. Asking somebody that's in the boat with you on what you should do does not make any sense. They are just as confused as you are, they have one paddle you got the other. Both of you drifting in the ocean with no direction but trying to lead the other to shore. It's an example of the blind leading the blind. Its nothing wrong with having someone to talk to, such as a mentor, but the mentor needs to be someone that's either where they want to be or where you would like to be.

It'll be a never-ending cycle if you allow needing someone else's approval become who you are, it will bind you, and in return it will bind your children. So, let's not give our children another cycle to break that we could have broken ourselves.

## Depression & Anxiety

Feeling rejected and casted out makes people feel alone and deserted. The want to do no wrong and the fear of doing wrong taunts the mind. Sometimes being anxious over what other people would consider little is massive to a person dealing with anxiety. Massive enough to cause anxiety attacks over something that seems small. Worrying about how they made themselves look in a situation or beating themselves up after making a mistake. A mistake that people on the outside may have forgotten all about but the anxiety attack we have in our room is because we feel as though people are shaming us and mocking us. Overthinking situations and becoming overwhelmed by what hasn't happened and probably never will. Wondering what people think of you and if they think you've made a fool of yourself.

It's a bunch of emotions that sparks depression and anxiety within a person and some don't know how to get through it. Some people seek for answers, and they don't feel as though they can find it because the problem goes so far back that the wounds are cut too deep. I say wounds because if it was a scar, it would mean healed. Things that are healed aren't suppressed under bandages, like how a person of depression hides their pain behind a smile. They don't feel loved, and if they experience rejection as a child, they weren't even taught love. They don't understand their emotions, so asking them to control them is telling someone to do something they've never done.

Depression can make people want to die, not everybody sees the light behind the dark room they confine themselves to. I remember even telling myself one day, "Shaunte' you have to open your blinds". I speak from experience, no I've never attempted suicide, but I've certainly felt dead inside. Not wanting to be around people, eating to feel better, feeling locked in my own mind. People deal with depression and anxiety different from others. No one's depression is the same as someone else's.

Rejection is a spirit and though we see it as one thing, it lives and recreates itself in different areas of our lives. The spirit of rejection runs havoc in a person's life, and it can drive them over the edge. Unfortunately, there's an ignorance to it, not everyone believes depression is real, some people think you can even snap out of it and even worse some think it's not a part of their culture. I told a relative of mine that I was depressed, and I was at a weak point in my life, and she told me "We don't get depressed, that's not our thing", pretty much told me I need to snap out of it because I'm strong. I can tell you right now a person that has suffered or is suffering from depression is tired of hearing how strong they are. I know it sounds like a compliment but it's a reminder of failure. "If I'm strong then how come I can't see it, what's wrong with me then, why do I feel this way?". Everybody is not looking to be strong all the time, it's a search for love, not strength.

There's so much I want to say about this topic, but I'm not a therapist. Everyone does not experience the same things therefore two depressions will not look the same. I recommend therapy to anyone who feels like they are depressed, and that anxiety is taking over their life. You have purpose here on earth and I would hate for anyone to feel that they no longer belong here. Suicide rates are high, especially in the crisis we are in right now with the pandemic. It has brought out so many emotions and people are struggling to stay positive. I pray strength over every person reading right now, God sees you and he hears you. Help is on the way. I come up against the spirit of depression that's in every reader and I bind and rebuke that demon in the name of Jesus.

Do not isolate yourself, it is the trick of the devil to get you alone. Surround yourself with love, pray & talk to Jesus. Invite the Holy Spirit into your life and allow God to give you a new heart. God can heal your depression and anxiety if you let him. Bring it to him in prayer, open up to Him and be honest, He already knows what you're carrying, but God gave us free will. He is a gentleman, He's not going to run up on you, He's going to knock, and you must let Him in. God knows what you are up against, and He will see you through, but you have got to open your mouth.

What is love? Teach me.

Did you know some people have never felt love, experienced love, don't know how to receive love, or give love? Love is taught, it's not something we are born knowing how to do. When a baby is born, the parents are told to practice skin to skin and other habits that will contribute to their child's mental and emotional needs. Babies need affection, love and attention in order to develop a sense of safety and security. Think about that, a growing child needs affection and attention in order to feel loved. If a newborn and/or child is neglected of such attention and affection they cry out until they are heard.

Each stage in life has its own cry for attention. Newborn's cry and its of course a normal thing and not looked down upon. Toddlers throw tantrums and though its often frowned upon its understandable. Teenagers act out, get into trouble at home and in school, and scream "I hate you" when they can't have their way. Adults, well sad to say some do throw tantrums, but the result of lack of love and affection is brought out in different ways, such as insecurities, low self-esteem, and toxicity in relationships whether they're the victim or the one guilty.

Some people are in relationships with people that just aren't capable of love and those relationships are doomed from the start. Sure, a person can teach their significant other love, but if the teacher is not patient and the learner is unaware of the root of their problem then class will end. Sometimes we must get to the root and heal before we can claim change. A starting point in that is praying on it. Simply asking God to show you what you need to work on will get you on the right track. Jesus is the best teacher and He's a healer; he sees things in you that you don't see in yourself. He sees the wounds, and he knows just how to make you clean. A healing process without Jesus is just wiping the surface. I learned that the hard way, I didn't need a dusting, I needed a new heart.

See, I didn't know how to give or receive love. Honestly, I'm still learning, but I'm better at it today than I was a year ago. Feeling rejected as a child did something to my heart that I wasn't aware of until I became an adult. I found out through anger and low self-esteem; a lot of times I was the toxic one. I would chase after people, whether family or men, that didn't love me while leaving behind and running away from those that did. I was conditioned to believe that what was toxic was love and what was love was abnormal. I thought someone showing they cared about me was them being clingy and soft. At one point I lost respect for men and had no care about their feelings, they were objects to me, and I treated them as such.

Rejection had shaped me to the point where I became the rejector and didn't even know it. It was rooted deep. I remember times where I didn't like to be touched, and it wasn't even a sexual touch just touched in general. I can't go as far to say maybe I wasn't held as a child, but I can tell you I wasn't loved on or shown affection as much as I needed. I grew up with my father and that side of the family was not affectionate at all, not even just towards me, in general it just wasn't a thing. There weren't hugs or "I love you" being tossed around often, if ever. We showed our love through jokes and sarcasm. My mother side of the family was more affectionate, so I knew it was a thing and I knew I was capable of it, however, being a victim of abuse and molestation, I wasn't receptive to it.

I didn't begin to learn how to love until I became a mother. Imagine that, being a mother of twins and not knowing how to love but having love for two infants all at once. In that moment I knew they needed me, and I was going to be there for them no matter. I had to learn how to pour emotions into them that I didn't feel poured into me. I just knew I couldn't let them feel how I felt, and I knew it had to start from the beginning. As my kids were growing day by day, so was I. I was going through something I didn't know how to express, and I suffered with post-partum because of it. I knew that God was tugging at my heart, and I had to surrender a lot of things because mentally and emotionally it was hard. Even though my kids' father was present, it didn't change the fact that I felt alone.

It's important for me to admit this to you so that you can understand the revelation I had in this. I was a mother, that didn't know what love was, trying to show two babies love without even knowing how to receive the love back that they were giving. There are so many parents, that don't know how to love, raising children, and those children grow up with the same lack their parents had. A lot of children are birthed by broken parents, and those parents can only do their best. Yes, parents that are self-ware know they have a cycle to break, I knew I had a cycle to break, but there are some parents that just don't know because they won't open their hearts to do the work.

I had to do what I knew was right until what I knew became a feeling of love to me. Motherly instincts are absolutely a thing, but what are your instincts as a mother? What was your example? Of course, I know how to kiss on my babies, hug them, tell them "I love you", and hold them when they cry. I also was in school studying brain development in a child, so actually, I was being schooled on what exactly they needed from me and how to give it to them. In the beginning I did it out of basic instinct and "this is what I'm going to do to make sure they feel it" but that was me learning throughout the first year of my children's life and I was mentally exhausted. It took a lot of time, healing and prayer, but now I can do it all because mommy feels like mommy. I had finally reached a point where not only can I teach them love, but I can give it to them.

## Discover Your Wounds

It was hard admitting that I had a problem. I knew that I was suffering from childhood trauma, but I didn't know how to categorize it. If we look at rejection and abandonment, we think that's our issue when really, it's the outcome. You don't just feel abandoned and rejected without a cause. Where did it stem from? You must find the direct problem in order to pull it up by its roots, and that my friend is where my healing began. Abuse, molestation, and feeling neglected was the root cause of my fear of rejection & abandonment, low self-esteem issues and insecurities.

Figuring out the root cause of your triggers and inner issues is discovered in soul searching. We must humble ourselves before God and ask him to expose us to ourselves. It sounds scary and it is, but He won't show you without guiding you through it. Actually, it's best that we do ask because when we don't try to work through it, we end up exposing ourselves to other people through our words and actions. Trust me, I'm speaking from experience.

I exposed all my unhealed trauma through my last relationship. Yes, unhealed wounds usually surface in romantic relationships. I believe it's because in those relationships we try to gain everything we've lacked, and we don't even know we're doing it. Its also in those time where we turn to God to ask him to deliver us from the pain and sometimes that person. I don't if you've ever been in a relationship that you knew wasn't healthy for you, but you just couldn't let go so you had to pray your way out of it. Yes, those are usually the ones because we want it so bad even though it's tearing us apart.

God knows where we are hurting, and He knows why. God is not pleased by the things that have hurt you, but He has not left you and He will never leave you nor forsake you. He will use your pain and turn it into a testimony, all things work together for your good.

Some of us are angry with God for allowing certain things to happen to us and we have hardened our hearts because of it. We can't see the root while we are stuck in the blame game. With Gods help you can dig deep and go back to what shook up your life. If you're angry, sad, hurt, confused, ask Him why, no matter the emotion, don't be ashamed. The devil wants us to shy away from God, making us feel ashamed for feelings things that aren't Holy, but God didn't come to save the perfect.

When I asked God to show me myself I did not like who I was. I was miserable, angry, full of hate and unforgiveness, I was disgusted with myself. I had let the things I went through shape who I was, and I did not like who I became. If we aren't careful, we'll use what happened to us as an excuse for how we act but "that's just how I am" is an ugly excuse. You are how you are because you refuse to change. We can't be out of our parents' house, grown and on our own still blaming things on them. At some point we must become responsible for our own actions and that starts with diving into the real problem.

You must go back to what hurt you and talk to your inner child. We can look at things and say oh it wasn't that bad with our adult mindset, but when you were that child, you didn't know how to handle that. Tell yourself that it's okay, that it wasn't your fault, and then forgive yourself for holding on to it for so long believing that it was.

It was not your fault that your parents couldn't accept you for who you were or didn't love you the way you needed to be loved.

It was not your fault that, that person couldn't keep their hands to themselves.

It was not your fault that they outcasted you and treated you like the black sheep.

It's not your fault that they can't see that you do matter.

It's not your fault that people didn't see the value in you.

It's not your fault that your father or mother walked out on you.

It's not your fault that addiction took over them.

It's not your fault your parents got a divorce.

Whatever it is speak it out loud, name it, and tell yourself that it is not your fault. The only fault in it is that you made the decision to carry it with you.

The reason why you need to name it is so you can speak directly to it. A doctor can't treat what they don't know you have, and you can't heal what you don't know you suffer from. Think of it as a tree. What you see is what came from the seed that was planted. Say you were abandoned as a child, the abandonment is the seed, the growth is fear of abandonment. You can't just say I have a fear of abandonment because where did it come from? Here's some examples.

I have a fear of abandonment because I was abandoned by my mother/father etc.

I have a fear of rejection because I was rejected by my family, and it made me feel unwanted.

I was molested as a child, so I feel insecure and have low self-esteem.

We tend to name things that are wrong with us, but never name the root of the problem, therefore, we try to heal what we won't acknowledge. You must dig it up in order to grab it by the root. You must go beyond the surface, or it'll just grow again, but when you pull the root, you kill the growth.

Think about when you see therapy sessions on tv or even if you've had therapy yourself. You tell them how you're feeling and what's going on in life and they always say "Tell me about your childhood, what was that like". There is a reason behind that, they know that what you are speaking of is not the root, but the problem. They are looking for the cause that made you have those results. You want to start at the end, but the therapist must take you to the beginning in order to get a better understanding. Ask yourself today, what are my issues the result of? Where did they come from? When you find the why, you'll be able to identify the source, heal it to starve it.

# The Glow Up

## Overcome Fear of Rejection

We all know that rejection hurts, and studies show that it activates the same part of the brain that physical pain does. We've already discussed that it can hold you back and that it can ruin your life if you let it. However, what if we changed the perspective on how you look at rejection? What if I told you rejection was a good thing?

When you get through the healing of your childhood and understanding what happened and what came from it. You can begin to see things differently because it'll be coming from a different perspective.

Rejection saves you from things you don't need, even if you think you need them or just have a want for them. Rejection is a no than can be perceived as a blessing in disguised when looking from healed eyes. Blind eyes and a broken heart only feels the pain and the emotions. A healed heart can hear wisdom over emotion and see the no as a redirection.

Let's start off with an example, when going to talk to someone you are attracted to, and they tell you "No", your feelings may be a little hurt, right? Well, instead of wondering why not, simply say "Okay" and walk away knowing that there was something down that path that wasn't for you. Allow the no to direct you elsewhere without your emotions holding you there. See, there's a lot of relationships and jobs that God has saved us from that would have been even worse than the ones we went and did anyway. We've dodged bullets that we didn't even know was flying in our vicinity because God stopped it. Sometimes you must see their "no" as God's warning. Think about your last relationship, if that person had said no, how many years would you have saved. I don't need the history behind it, it's an example to show you how a no could have saved you from the reroute you had to take if you didn't take the detour in the first place.

The "Okay" with no emotion's method can go with anything by simply seeing the bigger picture instead of doubting and blaming yourself. Not receiving a job after you went to an interview knowing you aced it and did all you could, can feel like a punch in the gut, but instead of saying "what did I do wrong, why didn't they like me?" say "Thank you, God. You moved this one out the way and I'm one step closer to the one you have for me". Now, this isn't for the people that halfway do things and say "welp, guess it wasn't meant to be" no, I'm not talking about you, this isn't your song. If you put your all into something, and get a no, that's a no for that thing, at that particular time, but it is not your excuse to stop pushing.

The home you tried to purchase or the apartment you tried to rent they told you no and you are devastated because you really wanted it. It's okay to be disappointed, but it's not okay to beat yourself up about it. Maybe if they had said yes, you wouldn't hear the Lord saying, "I have a better one just wait". I know we're talking about rejection, but somebody need to hear that you need to have patience too. The no is setting you up for God's best. Don't miss out on the blessing getting caught up in your emotions. The quickest way the devil get to you is through your mind, so if he can get you to create another rejection wound from a no, he will. He knows a harden heart will miss out on God and all he has for you.

If you have been bonded by rejection the devil will use it to destroy your mind. Confuse the enemy by changing the narrative, changing the narrative will change your story. A new story brings a different outcome all because of a change in perspective.

## Build Self Esteem

Self-esteem is very important and to build it requires dedicated to yourself. First, I would like to touch on self-awareness. Being self-aware is the ability to focus on yourself and understanding your internal standards. When you can understand your thoughts, actions and emotions, you can evaluate yourself. The saying look yourself in the mirror refers to your behavior but it's no point in that if you don't know how to align your behavior with your values.

I know people think its "crazy" to talk to yourself, but we all do it, just not out loud. Sometimes we need that one-on-one talk with ourselves to talk some sense into us or uplift us. Learn to listen to yourself, you know what you like and don't like, and if you don't, learn it. Be okay with taking yourself out and treating yourself to things. Get to know yourself how you would get to know someone else. Tune into your feelings, how do you feel when things happen. What makes you happy, what makes you sad? The reason why these things are important to building yourself esteem is because how can you build up self if you don't know self.

What is self-esteem? Self-esteem is your subjective evaluation of your own worth. So, if you don't even know who you are, then how do you know your worth? Spending time with yourself is a huge step in building your self-esteem. Some of us don't like to be alone because we are afraid of our thoughts, but that's where the self-awareness comes in again. Journaling is an amazing way to learn more about yourself. You can journal about whatever you want, most people journal about their day and their experiences. It's something you can look back on and see how far you've come.

When reading something you wrote months or even years ago you can easily see how much you've grown in that time. Journaling will help you release your feelings onto paper and become aware of your emotions in the things you write about.

Writing down "I am" statements, better known as affirmations, is also a great way to build self-esteem. For example, "I am beautiful", "I am smart", "I am enough", are some that, if said often, will create confidence. You say it until you believe it. You are telling yourself what you are even if you don't feel like it, until you believe it to be true. I believe that affirmations are best done in the mirror. Looking yourself right in the eyes and reminding yourself of who you are is a beautiful thing. Don't be afraid to look at yourself and accept everything about you, flaws and all. You were created by the Most High God, in his own image, you are just how God imaged and created you to be. There is no other you, you are the original, hand crafted by the creator, there is no mistake on you.

Taking yourself out on a date is another type of self-love, self-care, that I personally love and enjoy. I remember when I was a waitress at a fancy steakhouse restaurant, I would always see people come in to eat alone. I felt bad for them, I assumed they were alone and had no one, especially the older ones. Little did I know they had it figured it. It's no better company than yourself, and if you can't stand to be alone with you then you must realize no one else will want too either. Being able to take yourself out is getting to know you, it honestly should be one of your best dates. You know what you like, and it's nobody there to get on your nerves but you.

A beautiful date night for yourself is so underrated. There is so much peace and love in getting yourself dressed and sexy for you. Put on the dress you've been wanting to wear, perfume, your favorite heels and take yourself to your favorite restaurant. Sit down at the table of your choice, order your glass of wine, with your favorite entrée and eat in peace. Take your time and enjoy the moment. The reason why this important is because you are teaching yourself what you like and what you would like to receive. Men, this goes for you too, there's nothing wrong with putting on your favorite suit and taking yourself out to your favorite restaurant either.

Little did I know the person that was at the table for one was no lonelier than the person sitting at a table for two. Just because they were alone didn't mean they were lonely, but sometimes the woman at the table with her man was, but that's a whole other story. When I tell you after learning that, I wasted no time in taking myself out and it was amazing. The confidence you give yourself after showing love to yourself is beautiful. You may not like it at first, may seem a little weird and awkward but the reward in it is so worth it.

Take the time to unlearn what society has taught you. Take time to undo what has made you feel any less than what and who you are. You owe it to yourself to be the woman you've dreamed of being. Unfortunately for most of us, it involves detoxifying ourselves from what other people have told us about us. Things may have happened to us that has made us feel unclean and unworthy, but those things do not become us. We have the victory over it all and we shall come out victorious. We are beautiful on the outside, and with prayer and healing we become beautiful on the inside as well.

## Take Care of Yourself

Now, I know that putting yourself first is something that a lot of people struggle with, but it's not up for a debate. You need to put yourself first. Stop putting yourself on the back burner while everyone else get what they need out of you. Too many times people around you drain you to the point where you have no energy left for yourself. Especially, us moms, I have two four-year old's so trust me, I know. You honestly can't even go to the bathroom without being needed. So, you have to make a point to put yourself first, or you won't be able to give 100 percent, because you won't be at 100 percent.

Whether it's your job, your spouse, the kids, whomever or whatever is taking your time, you must first give yourself some time. What I mean is in the morning before the show starts, give yourself an hour that's all about you. Wake up before everyone else, spend some time with God, make your coffee, exercise, take your nice hot shower, do your skin care routine, and pull yourself together. You will find that when you give yourself some quiet time in the morning to take care of you first, you'll have the energy when everyone else wakes up asking you a billion questions.

I find that having something to look forward to also helps me. It could be my favorite desert after dinner or just a night in with the kids watching a movie. Anything that lift your spirits is part of taking care of you. Even sitting in your car to get your mind right after work before you go in the house is something I consider self-care. That little time to get your thoughts together and steal some peace and quiet is important.

To go along with the mind, of course, we must mention the body. It's time to start the healthy eating we keep putting off until next month that somehow ends up becoming a new year's resolution. Let's not forget the gym sessions we promised ourselves either. Now, I'm not going to lie to you, I fall short of this myself. I'm still working on losing the same 40lbs I was supposed to lose 2 years ago, but that's neither here nor there.

Once we feel good about ourselves, we will start to carry ourselves better. Seeing the person, we desire to be when we look in the mirror is a confidence booster. However, don't confuse getting healthy with becoming beautiful. You're already beautiful, you're just reaching the mind and body goal you have set for yourself, if you have one to begin with.

I know everyone has their differences on how they pull themselves together. Some women desire to be natural, no make-up, no wigs and extensions as well as there are women that do enjoy make up, wigs etc. It's nothing wrong with neither, I personally enjoy doing both. Part of taking care of yourself is doing what makes you feel good. You can wake up and not feel good or feel like yourself but the moment you begin to do your hair and put on some lipstick you'll feel your mood change almost instantly.

I know there's a saying of "Don't let yourself go" and I know there has been a debate on what that means but allow it to mean whatever it means to you, for you. Don't stop doing what makes you feel like you. Rolling out of bed, barely brushing your teeth, not touching your hair, throwing on a t-shirt full of holes and jeans with bleach stains because you wore them to clean the toilet is a look, we can all agree to say "Whew, honey, no". However, going from wearing make up to no longer wearing make up to dressing up every day to wanting to wear comfortable jeans is not letting yourself go. It's ok to find the style and look that fits you and make you feel good. It's all about what makes you happy in your own skin.

Your mental, physical and spiritual health is important, and it needs to be catered to, in order to always keep you at one hundred percent. Go see your doctor, take care of your body. See your therapist, it's nothing wrong with it even if you think you're fine having someone to help you through life is a blessing. Most importantly, prayer, build your one-on-one relationship with God. He will give you the kind of peace and joy the world never will.

## Create Healthy Relationships

Once you have started your healing process and begun to get to know yourself you will notice a change in your relationships. Your friendships, relationships with family and your romantic relationships will not be the same, and that's what you want. You want to see the difference in how you interact with people in your life and new people you will meet along the way. It will show you how much you have changed and that's the point, change.

You would have learned to create boundaries as a part of getting to know yourself; knowing your likes and dislikes along with what you will and will not tolerate. As you meet people you will be able to discern whether they will fit into your life or not. You will not be easily persuaded into friendships and relationships that do not have your best interest. When being secure in who you are, you will not feel the need to hold on to people that aren't good for you. The newfound love and respect you have for yourself will keep you from making decisions based on rejection and abandonment.

Friendships will be healthy relationships with people that are mentally mature, positive, supportive and loving, coming from you and them. You will no longer be willing to tolerate friends that are selfish and of toxic ways. Honestly, you will begin to see your circle smaller because a lot of people won't grow with you. You will find yourself leaving a lot of friendships behind and that's ok. Part of the process is learning what friendships are for you and which ones aren't.

Making new friends won't be as hard as it seems anymore either. I know people think that making friends in our adult years is a little awkward sometimes, but you'll find that once you walk in your purpose the people you need around you will fall into place. You will begin meeting people that have the same interests as you. Allow yourself to be approachable at events and gatherings. Being authentically you will draw in people that fit well with your personality. You don't have to throw yourself out there, just be genuine and watch God bring people to you.

Family members will notice a change in you as well and because they too are human, title or not, some will stay, and some will go. Finding yourself means, again, learning what you will and will not tolerate. To be honest, a lot of family members cross boundaries just because they believe they can. However, the person you have glowed up to be will stand up for yourself whether cousin, auntie, uncle or whomever likes it or not. Sometimes our most toxic relationships are within our family because we feel loyal to them which allows them to hurt us repeatedly because we choose to continue to come around. Some will respect the healthy and improved you, and some won't. Some people enjoy the broken you better because the broken you didn't stand for anything. Know they can mean well, but they can mean well at a distance if that's what is healthy for you.

You will notice that you are a better mother, daughter, sister etc. You will be able to communicate better. When conversing with people listen to understand and not just to respond. Hurt people want to get their point across, healed people know that two people can have different opinions and still learn from it. Take time to listen to your children, they are people that are too filled will emotions, with their own personalities and need you treat them with respect. Yes, children need and deserve respect, just as much as adults.

Now, when it comes to getting back on the dating scene, it'll be completely new to you now. The best way to create a healthy romantic relationship is to not rush it. Give yourself time to learn about the person, do not jump over the dating process. Remember, we must first heal, get to know ourselves and be content with being alone first, before we run off looking for love. When you take the necessary time, you'll realize it's not necessary or even smart, to rush. Actually, we'll begin to see that we don't have to go searching after all. It's when we get to our place of healing, learning our self-worth and walking in our purpose that the Lord will open the door to meet our kingdom spouse. He who finds a wife, finds a great thing, you will be sought after. Stop the chase.

If you are still living a rejection-based lifestyle, easily moved and persuaded, chasing love to fill abandonment issues you will continuously be hurt by men on purpose. There are men that seek out women that don't know their worth, just to use them up and have their way. A man can only do what you allow. Have you ever told somebody what you've gone through and how others have hurt you and that person turned around and did the same thing? That's because you told them what you were willing to tolerate, so if they don't do more than that you'll stay.

In order to be in the dating scene, you must be confident, self-aware and have boundaries. Know what you want in life and have direction. When you know where you are going, you'll be more conscious about the person you decide to date because if you are truly about accomplishing your life plan you won't tolerate someone trying to take you on a different route. You won't allow someone to waste your time, because you'll know how valuable time is, and wasted time is not something you can get back. So, if you go on a date with a man and he has no priorities, goals or simply don't match with you, you won't try to force it because you are on different paths in life.

Be confident enough to know there's someone else out there. Confidence is a sexy thing on anybody. It's something beautiful about a person knowing their worth. So glad we dropped the insecurities a few chapters ago because now we can walk with our head high.  Confidence is something a man pays attention to; a man can smell insecurities a mile away and the wrong man will take advantage of it. The only way to date healthy is to be mentally ready, not perfect, but ready. Dating while broken is going to get you broken hearted. For example, if a man tells you something that goes against your boundaries, and you switch up your beliefs just to keep him around you're not ready.

Trust yourself enough to trust your intuition. If you know after the first date that the answer is "no, not the one" then you don't owe him anything other than to not waste his time or yours. If he knows after the first date that you aren't for him, accept his rejection as a blessing. Just because he's a good man does not mean he's good for you. Understand you are not the only one that can walk away from this potential relationship, so don't be taken back if he decides to move on.

Healthy dating is getting to know each other and creating a bond that is respectful to the both of you. Your feelings are not more important than his and his feelings are not more important than yours. However, neither of you should feel the need to have to give up their boundaries. I am not talking about reasonable sacrifices; I'm talking about boundaries. For example, if you do not want to have sex with him, you do not have to and if he feels like he can't go any further with you because you refuse to, then let him know that it was nice meeting him and remove yourself. Again, that's why we don't date insecure or with abandonment issues, because something like that would have a rejection-based dater rethinking everything. I'll give you another example, if you are two-three dates in, by now this should have come up, and he says I don't want kids, and you know in your heart that you do, it is not your place to try to change his mind. Let him know that that's not something you are willing to change your mind on, tell him you had a great time and move on.

The decisions you've made in the past are based on the choices you've had in front of you. Whether you chose right or wrong is for you to determine. Based on your past relationships, did you make healthy choices? Did you give in on things you told yourself you wouldn't? Did you allow things you told yourself you'd never allow? Those are the decisions we made with the choices at hand. Were they good or bad?

So, let's say the dating is going well and the two of you decide to become a couple. Great. God first, healthy communication, respect, support, understanding each other and love will create a thriving healthy relationship. However, know that even in your relationship there's still lines that should not be crossed. What it took to get each other does not end just because you have each other. You still have to keep up with the things mentioned above along with expressing love to one another. However, don't confuse love with having to accept things that are unacceptable. You still must love yourself enough to walk away when you know that you should.

The reason people need to come together after they've begun healing from the past hurt and childhood traumas is because in relationships things that aren't healed will resurface. It happens every time and there's no escaping it. Heal from your last relationship so that the new person doesn't have to take on the burden of it. It's not fair to the person you're with to have to deal with the last persons mistakes. Control and trust issues are not of a healthy relationship. That is the type of toxicity society has conditioned us to allow, break it.

Give yourself the chance to experience true and healthy love. Ask God to show you how to love that person. It may be your first healthy relationship, so it all may be new to you. Remember this relationship is the one after your healing, it's not going to be like any relationship you've had in the past. You are a lot calmer now, there's no baggage with pain, insecurities and trust issues packed inside. No one has dated this version of you before, so take your time. Have fun and enjoy the ride, but remember, you're not just hopping on any ride, know the destination.

## What is Your Life Plan?

Write it down and make it plain, not only is that in the bible, but it was also the words the Lord said to me. Yes, the Lord has a plan for us, however he also allows us free will and gives us the desires of our heart according to his plan. We can't be too focused on our plan that we miss God and what he has for us. So, if we give our plans to God and allow him to purify them, because it's for God's glory and not our own, he will give it back to us and order our steps along the way.

Having a plan will keep you focused and on the right path. When you know your purpose, your gift, what you are here on earth to do, put it to work. Write down your goals and the timeline you would like to achieve them. Break each goal down step by step and give it it's on deadline. That will help keep you from getting overwhelmed. When you see a deadline with a lot of work, anxiety can have us not knowing where to start, and usually that results in us not starting at all.

Writing a plan will again, raise your standards and create boundaries for you. When you have direction it's hard to be thrown off your route. You won't fall for anything or anyone that will cause you to get off track. When you know you have somewhere to go and somewhere to be, you will not allow those distractions anymore. Time will be far too valuable to you once you know how to use it wisely.

After you write a plan, you must follow it, or it simply won't work. No, it will not look just like you wrote it, it will not go exactly as you planned. However, writing a plan is not to just make you look good in the eyes of others. It's best to keep your plans to yourself, keeping people out of your business will benefit you. Following the plan simply means do not waiver from it and do not forget it. Read it, every day, and try not to put everything off on tomorrow. Be careful with outside opinions, don't let people tell you what won't work; just because it didn't work for them does not mean it will not work for you.

Your plan is your baby and just like a baby you must protect it, take care of it and nurture it. Only give birth to your plan when its ready. Notice I said when it's ready and not exactly when you are ready. Sometimes we like to trick ourselves into thinking we aren't ready when in fact we are ready. Releasing it when it's premature is risky, but whatever it is will thrive with a thought-out plan, determination and God's approval.

## Glow Victoriously

The entire mission of this book is to help you heal and grow into the next level. Becoming a better you have always been a thought in your mind, but you never really knew what was holding you back or didn't know where to start. We now know that starting from the root of your problem is the first step to your healing. You deserve to be the women you dream of, and you will become her, all you needed was a push.

You are no longer a victim, you are victorious. You have overcome your past and the traumas that came with it. Years of pain, guilt & shame has tried to tear you down and take you out, but it only made you stronger. Allowing yourself to live and be set free is an amazing gift to give yourself. You have learned to love yourself, grow spiritually and mentally. You've also learned create boundaries and standards and the importance of doing so. This has been a journey for you, and it will not end here. No, you may not be at your one hundred percent, but at least now you know where to start.

God is good, and he will set you free from all that has you bound. God saved me from the spirit of rejection and abandonment. It was ruining my life until I learned that my actions and emotions was coming from a hurt place. It took me getting into a relationship that triggered all my childhood traumas to understand that my inner child was still suffering. I thought I had forgiven those that hurt me until it came out screaming. It took a lot out of me and finding myself had to become my focus. Allowing God to take me to the root was not easy and it hurt like crazy. However, if God led me to it, I knew he would lead me through it. I didn't want to face my past alone, and it took a lot of tears, frustration, and anger, before I realized I was never alone after all.

Surrendering it all to God and allowing him to do the work in you will save you from the search. Trust me, God has a way of showing us what we need to know and improve. However, the best part of that is when the Lord leads us to what needs to be healed, he delivers us from it, and sets us completely free.

You will not be perfect, none of us ever will be, but you will feel healthier and happier. The physical damage your emotions has caused will no longer weigh on your body. Your mind will be at ease, and you will be able to focus on what really matters to you. You owe it to yourself to gain your life back, it's time to take back everything the devil stole from you.

The Lord will restore your faith and give you a new heart. It's time to let him in, you've tried everything else, you've already tried doing it your way. I ran until I was exhausted, don't be like me. When the Lord knocks, let him in, you don't have to healed before surrendering yourself to him. He can use you just the way you are. Take the steps to unharden your heart. Feeling rejected by people will make us think that God will reject us too and that's not true. Open your heart to receive not only God, but the changes in you. Give yourself a chance to heal victoriously, you deserve it.

Dear Lord Jesus, I know that I am a sinner, and I ask for Your forgiveness. I believe You died for my sins and rose from the dead. I turn from my sins and invite You to come into my heart and life. I want to trust and follow You as my Lord and Savior. In Jesus name, Amen.